Other 'crazy' gigglebooks by Bill Stott

Sex – it drives us crazy!

Marriage – it drives us crazy!

Football – it drives us crazy!

Cats – they drive us crazy!

Computers – they drive us crazy!

Published simultaneously in 2007 by Helen Exley Giftbooks in Great Britain, and Helen Exley Giftbooks LLC in the USA

12 11 10 9 8 7 6 5 4 3 2 1

Selection and arrangement copyright © 2007 Helen Exley
Cartoons copyright © 2007 Bill Stott

ISBN 13: 978-1-84634-133-5

A copy of the CIP data is available from the British Library on request.

Edited by Gayle Morgan and Helen Exley

Printed in China

Helen Exley Giftbooks, 16 Chalk Hill, Watford, Herts, WD19 4BG, UK
Helen Exley Giftbooks LLC, 185 Main Street, Spencer MA 01562, USA
www.helenexleygiftbooks.com

Golf

IT
DRIVES
US CRAZY!

A HELEN EXLEY GIGGLEBOOK

CARTOONS
BY BILL STOTT

"Don't mind me – carry on –
I've got to a good bit."

"Terry's so naturally gifted, he has to make everything impossible...."

"This really is most sporting of you...."

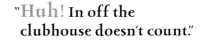

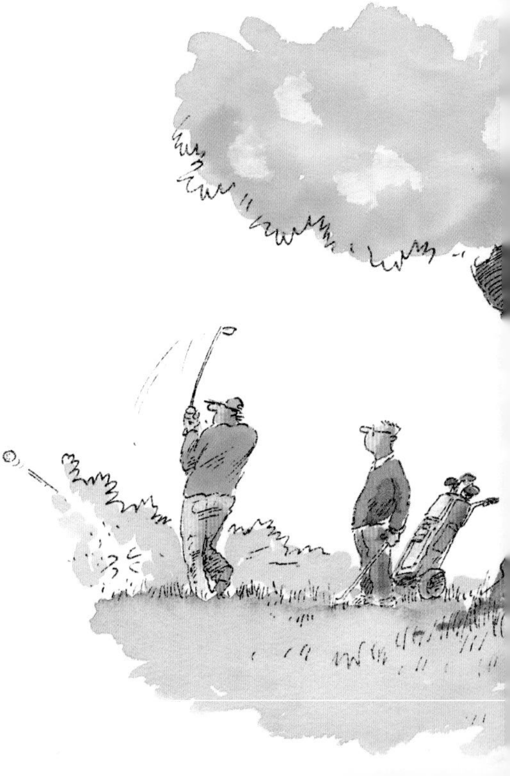

"The big ones with the sticks are at war with the little round white ones...."

"Cobalt treated titanium... Solid cast, with a unique layer of poly-dylibdenum.

1

Cost the earth, and makes no
difference whatsoever."

2

"Every club has its traditionalist...."

"He just never knows when he's beaten...."

"Eighty-five and still loads of enthusiasm for the game, but a diminished sense of direction...."

"Never mind – you're on the green in two...."

"Ahh! This is the life...."

FORE!

"At 47 over par, he needs the long-range battery...."

"Ingenious, but sadly, illegal too."

"Normally, that's a good shot, but considering the fact that you hit it, it's a brilliant shot."

"Mr Finnington – almost anyone can learn to play golf. Unfortunately – you're an almost."

"Head down. Bring that shoulder around.
Bend the knees... left hand up."

1

"OK. How does that feel?"

"OK, heads we go husky sledding in Alaska,
or tails I renew my golf club membership."

"I'm good at golf. I can feel it inside me.
It just never comes out while I'm playing."

"Now, if you were a golf ball,
where would **you** hide?"

"No Audrey I will not concede.
Now hold that torch steady."

About Bill Stott

Bill Stott is a freelance cartoonist whose work never fails to pinpoint the absurd and simply daft moments in our daily lives. Originally Head of Arts faculty at a city high school, Bill launched himself as a freelance cartoonist in 1976. With sales of 2.8 million books with Helen Exley Giftbooks, Bill has an impressive portfolio of 26 published titles, including his very successful *Spread of Over 40s' Jokes* and *Triumph of Over 50s' Jokes*.

Bill's work appears in many publications and magazines, ranging from the *The Times Educational Supplement* to *Practical Poultry*. An acclaimed after-dinner speaker, Bill subjects his audience to a generous helping of his wit and wisdom, illustrated with cartoons drawn deftly on the spot!

What is a Helen Exley giftbook?

We hope you enjoy *Golf – it drives us crazy!* It's just one of many hilarious cartoon books available from Helen Exley Giftbooks, all of which make special gifts. We try our best to bring you the funniest jokes because we want every book we publish to be great to give, great to receive.

HELEN EXLEY GIFTBOOKS creates gifts for all special occasions – not just birthdays, anniversaries and weddings, but for those times when you just want to say 'thanks' or make someone laugh. Why not visit our website, www. helenexleygiftbooks.com, and browse through all our gift ideas?

ALSO BY BILL STOTT
Marriage – it drives us crazy!
Cats – they drive us crazy!
Football – it drives us crazy!
Sex – it drives us crazy!
Computers – they drives us crazy!

Information on all our titles is also available from
Helen Exley Giftbooks, 16 Chalk Hill, Watford WD19 4BG, UK.
Helen Exley Giftbooks LLC, 185 Main Street, Spencer MA 01562, USA.
www.helenexleygiftbooks.com